Co-Parenting A Toxic Ex

How To Survive Co-Parenting With a Narcissist And Raise Resilient Children

Ruby Eden

Copyright©Ruby Eden

All Rights Reserved

TABLE OF CONTENTS

INTRODUCTION

CHAPTER ONE
- Who Is a Narcissist?
  - Challenges Of Co-Parenting With a Narcissist
  - Seven Definite Indicators That Your Co-Parent Is a Narcissist
  - How To Spot a Narcissist
  - How To Survive Co-Parenting With a Narcissist
  - How to Set Boundaries when Co-Parenting with a Narcissist

CHAPTER TWO
- Parental Alienation Syndrome
  - Parental Alienation Syndrome Signs And Symptoms
  - Signs That Parental Alienation May Be Taking Place
  - How Parental Alienation Affects Children
  - How To Overcome Parental Alienation: Reestablishing Contact With Your Children

CHAPTER THREE
- How to Support Your Children When Their Parent Is Narcissistic
  - How To Protect Your Children From a Parent Who Is a Narcissist

CHAPTER FOUR
- How To Help Your Kid Become Resilient While Co-Parenting With a Narcissist
  - Resilience Is Crucial While Co-Parenting With a Narcissist.

INTRODUCTION

Even for the most amicable ex-partners, co-parenting is often a difficult task. However, co-parenting with a narcissist may become very difficult. Even if you no longer share a residence with your narcissistic ex, you are still connected to them via your children, thus understanding how to co-parent with a narcissist will help you establish boundaries and maintain equilibrium and sanity.

Certain actions have been linked to narcissistic co-parents. These actions include exaggerating one's importance, lying, assigning blame, gaslighting, gossiping, criticizing, and similar things. These actions not only harm your relationship, but they may also place the kids in a difficult position. When the warning indicators are discovered, there are strategies you may use to cope with them and defend yourself from the narcissistic co-parent.

CHAPTER ONE

Who Is a Narcissist?

The self-worth and self-image of those who suffer from a narcissistic personality disorder (NPD) are overblown. They don't have empathy or sympathy for others and constantly put their wants first. A narcissist demands excessive attention and craves the admiration of others. They often assign responsibility for their faults and shortcomings to others.

Many people who suffer from narcissistic personality disorder were raised in unhappy environments and learned to deal by believing they were better than everyone else. They did, however, also become hypersensitive to remarks, disapproval, and desertion.

Narcissists often exhibit abrupt mood swings, impulsive conduct, and violent outbursts. In partnerships, they are often abusive, manipulative, or dominating.

Even if a person does not have a narcissistic personality disorder, they may nonetheless exhibit narcissistic personality characteristics that sometimes make co-parenting problematic.

Challenges Of Co-Parenting With a Narcissist

Cooperation, understanding, and collaboration are necessary for co-parenting. But narcissists often have an exaggerated sense of their significance and a basic lack of empathy. Therefore, it could be difficult for you to work together with your narcissistic ex when it comes to co-parenting.

After you exit a toxic relationship, your ex could believe that it is okay to continue to dominate, bully, or otherwise abuse you. It's common for narcissists to think they are above the law and that the laws don't apply to them. Expecting your narcissistic ex to co-parent in a healthy and mutually rewarding manner is unrealistic since they always feel like victims.

It may be difficult to co-parent with a narcissist for a variety of reasons, including:

- They could decline to consent to custody.
- A narcissist could not consent to the terms of a court order.
- By telling you how much they miss you and your family, they could attempt to influence you.
- Your narcissistic ex-partner could trespass on your personal space and disrupt your kid's schedule.
- To keep control, they could engage in triangulation and entice children into your relationship.
- They could attempt to incite children to hate you.

Seven Definite Indicators That Your Co-Parent Is a Narcissist

It can be challenging to raise kids when a couple is no longer together. However, when you're truly co-parenting with an egotistical person, the issue gets a lot worse. To effectively co-parent with narcissistic people, it's critical to understand their behavior. But first, you'd need to be aware of the symptoms.

Certain actions have been linked to narcissistic co-parents. These actions include exaggerating one's importance, lying, assigning blame, gaslighting, gossiping, criticizing, and similar things. These actions not only harm your relationship, but they may also put the kids in a difficult situation. When the warning indicators are discovered, there are strategies you may use to deal with them and defend yourself from the narcissistic co-parent.

How to Spot a Narcissist

1. They Believe They Are Unique

The personality characteristic known as narcissism is characterized by self-involvement, selfishness, a lack of empathy for others, and a craving for adulation. It is named after the mythological character who stared at himself nonstop until he passed away. With this concept, it is simple to understand why narcissistic individuals might overestimate their specialness. Relationships with these people are particularly difficult because they frequently only show themselves, love. Co-parenting is already a challenging task, and narcissistic personalities only serve to exacerbate this difficulty.

2. They Mislead You

It's likely that if you co-parent with a narcissist, you have discovered that they frequently lie to you. A narcissist is not honest; rather, what distinguishes them is their self-centeredness. Because the commitments they make don't mean that much to them, they frequently lie to the people around them. If it prevents them from being yelled at, they will tell you what they think you want to hear rather than the truth.

The worst aspect of narcissists' lies is when they are told to kids. These narcissists are capable of telling their children something significant, such as, "I'll be there for your big game," and then entirely forgetting it the following day.

Because it might be risky to raise a child with a co-parent who does not give you the full picture, it is crucial to be alert to this indicator.

3. They never admit mistakes

Narcissists believe they are the center of the universe, hence they are incapable of doing anything wrong. Unfortunately, that means they'll always try to blame you for anything. Whose fault is the child's declining grade? Who is to blame if no one picked up the child from school? Regardless of what you've already talked about, you'll frequently find your co-parent pointing a finger at you.

It can be very challenging to co-parent with someone who constantly assigns blame, especially when the child is caught in the midst. For instance, the co-parent accused you of failing to not remind them about the child's talent presentation when they weren't able to make it. If your co-parent's accusations are heard by your child, it makes it even harder for them because they are already upset by the parent's absence.

4. They Gaslight You

In addition to the previous point, narcissists frequently shift responsibility by gaslighting others. Mental manipulation known as "gaslighting" is frequent in unhealthy relationships. It is a method of communication that modifies the story and causes you to doubt yourself.

Say, for illustration, that your co-parent failed to pick up your child from daycare over the weekend. You give them a call and remind them of your prior agreement.

You can be gaslighted by your narcissistic co-parent by hearing yourself say, "You must be crazy. That conversation was never had by us! This is how it always is. You always portray me as the villain even though I haven't done anything wrong.

If you're successful, you might heed their advice and reflect on how you've treated them in the past. But in reality, all they're doing is controlling you. Gaslighting reframes the problem and paints you as the bad guy in every situation.

5. They Whisper to Your Back

Ex-narcissists don't respect you very much. This means that when you learn later that they are truly talking negatively about you, it won't come as a surprise to you. To their friends and family, perhaps. Since your ex's remarks can alter how your friends perceive you, it can even become harmful if they speak negatively about you behind your back to shared friends. The worst scenario, though, is when they mention you to the kids.

When co-parents are not respectful of one another, it is not unusual to hear one co-parent speak poorly of the other to the children. This is particularly true for co-parents who are narcissists since they want the kids to like them more than you do. As a result, they use a variety of strategies to strengthen their argument. For instance, they don't correct the kids even when they did something wrong to make you seem like a scary parent. The worst possible amount of negative chatter about you is one of these tricks.

6. They Dismiss You

Some narcissistic co-parents would criticize you in front of you and then immediately speak behind your back. These narcissists will be honest with you when they believe you have erred since they believe they are the perfect parents who can do no wrong. When they perform this in front of other people, it is very embarrassing. Their ego prevents them from empathizing; in fact, they want a crowd to hear them criticize you to demonstrate how superior they are to you.

When narcissistic co-parents attack you in front of the children, this is very difficult. You undoubtedly go above and beyond as a parent to offer your children the greatest possible existence. However, it might unintentionally sow the seeds of doubt in a child's mind when a parent criticizes another parent in front of the youngster. This may cause children to reflect on their situation and consider whether one parent is superior to the other.

7. The Kids Are Isolated

Because they are so self-centered, narcissistic co-parents frequently keep the kids to themselves. This indicates that they frequently keep kids away from friends and family who they don't like. This may give your kids an erroneous impression about the people in your life, which can be quite detrimental to their social development.

If you give in to their demands, they may develop a more extreme kind of possessiveness, which will make it very challenging to co-parent with them.

How To Survive Co-Parenting With a Narcissist

If there is no abuse or any other substantial reason to keep your narcissistic ex away from children, it is helpful to discover a strategy to co-parent with a narcissist and make the situation bearable at least. Here are some suggestions that may assist you.

1. Establish a legal parenting plan

Narcissists may want to be in the picture as much as practical. If you develop a formal parenting plan or custody agreement, you'll have everything on paper. That way, if your ex starts seeking more time or wants to manipulate certain conditions, it's enforced by a person outside your relationship.

A plan might address issues like who pays for medical expenditures (or who pays what percentage), visiting arrangements for daily life, and visitation dates for holidays. Whatever is included under your custody agreement should be set out and unambiguous so there are absolutely no gray areas that may be misused.

Talking with a lawyer is an expenditure, but building a legal plan may assist throughout the balance of your co-parenting years.

2. Make use of court services

A guardian ad litem (GAL) is a court-appointed (neutral) person who looks out for the "best interest of a child." You may request that one be appointed.

The guardian becomes familiar with your kid and their condition and gives suggestions to the court based on their requirements. Concerning co-parenting, this may address considerations like where your child will spend most of their time or how much interaction a youngster should have with each parent.

Mediators, on the other hand, operate as a go-between for communication and settlement between parents. In some nations, they are a required component in custody disputes while in others their participation is elective.

They may assist resolve any difficulties that got you and your ex to court. They do not give commands or suggestions. Instead, parents establish the parenting plan while working with mediators. Then this plan is brought before a judge and eventually becomes court-ordered.

3. Maintain stringent limitations

Narcissists thrive on the experiences they obtain from others - whether favorable or detrimental. Setting up limitations is a technique that may decrease your ex's power to get you fired up.

For example, you may suggest that you talk entirely via text or email. That way, you have some time to respond before you reply to requests and other communications coming your way. It also helps you with documentation.

These constraints could apply to your ex's connection with your child as well. If your court-ordered agreement allows, try specifying specific hours when your ex may phone to contact your child during visitations. And clutch to your weaponry. The narcissist may not respond well to having limitations established at first, but — with time — you'll learn they're essential and oh-so useful.

4. Parent with empathy

It may be hard to avoid getting caught up in the dramatics of co-parenting, but try your best to remember your child among all this. Parenting with empathy requires putting yourself in your child's shoes and responding to circumstances in ways that take their feelings completely into account.

You may also teach your youngster to comprehend their feelings — whether that's sorrow, irritation, or rage. If kids know what they're experiencing, they can better communicate about it and navigate through challenging moments. And keep in mind that your child is likely not getting this type of positive modeling or understanding from their narcissistic parent, so it's doubly crucial.

5. Avoid speaking ill of the other co-parent in front of the kids

Along with this, it's a good idea to keep fights with your ex and specific name-calling or other complaints to yourself (or potentially a trusted friend, family member, or therapist) (or perhaps a trusted friend, family member, or therapist) (or perhaps a trusted friend, family member, or therapist) (or perhaps a trusted friend, family member, or therapist) (or perhaps a trusted friend, family member, or therapist). Ranting just places your tiny one in the middle of something they didn't ask to be a part of. It produces tension and the difficulties of picking sides.

6. Avoid emotional arguments

Your ex is likely to revel in seeing you very terrified or uncomfortable. Don't give them pleasure. And when it comes to arguments, resist using your child as a go-between, negotiator, or to otherwise gather information.

If this is particularly hard for you to grasp, consider seeing your interactions with your ex like a job. You must not agree on everything, but you do have to work together. This strategy may help you push through tense talks and keep the argument to a minimum.

7. Expect challenges

Reframing your expectations may also assist. If you enter into different parenting circumstances anticipating some resistance, you may be less astonished or terrified when issues materialize. Alternatively, you may feel pleasantly thrilled if something goes through particularly nicely.

Remember: Co-parenting may be tough even if parents are normally pleasant. While some circumstances may be made more unpleasant working with a narcissist, some of it is just part of adapting to the new normal.

8. Document everything

Write everything down. Or establish a digital notebook of stuff you feel is noteworthy. These might include the dates and times when your ex won't deliver the agreed-upon visitation or any abuse/neglect you suspect. Anything that doesn't look right or isn't being done as you've agreed should be documented if you wish to take action on it.

You may even choose to recruit an impartial someone (a neighbor, for example) to serve as a witness to what you're claiming, including late or missing pick-ups/drop-offs. All the proof you obtain may be employed in court to help you with custody. No detail is too trivial.

9. Consider counseling

If it's starting to be too much to bear on your own, scream out. A trained therapist can help you work through issues and come to solutions for those exceedingly challenging situations. Even just talking about your views with neutral individuals can help you take a step back and analyze your stance.

And counseling isn't an awful alternative for your child either. Your child's ideas regarding divorce are likely different from your own. You may attempt to locate organizations via your local school or community for children of divorce. Beyond that, if you believe your little one is acting out or having a horrible time, contact your physician for a referral to a child or teen therapist.

10. Maintain perspective on disputes

Even under the worst conditions, be mindful to know what you're up against. Underneath that façade of obvious confidence, the narcissist is quite sensitive to criticism and typically has very poor self-esteem. Your arguments are much less about the issues at hand and far more about ego.

Knowing this is half the effort. What's vital is that you keep sanity and your youngster stays safe. Advocate for your kid and keep their interests nearest to your heart. In the long run, shutting the spotlight off all the spats and focussing your attention on what's genuinely vital can only enhance your relationship with your kids.

11. Build a Support System

To restore confidence and increase mood, surround yourself with the people who love you and understand you. Although you don't have to express your co-parenting problems if you don't feel comfortable disclosing the truth, it helps to know that your loved ones are supporting you.

12. Practice Self-Care

Co-parenting with a narcissist may be stressful. So, don't forget to put self-care as a priority. Make sure you eat correctly and get enough sleep daily. Exercise, practice mindfulness, and go on long walks in nature. Spend t me with positive people, practice appreciation, and keep a diary of your thoughts and feelings. These fundamental self-care routines may help you deal with stress, increase your mood, and make you feel safe.

13. Talk to Your Children

One of the most critical things you need to do when you've determined you're co-parenting with a narcissist is to discuss it with your kids. Having divided parents is difficult enough, there's no need to make it tougher for them by being in a stressful co-parenting situation.

It may take some time, but youngsters could inevitably pick up on the narcissist co-parent's dishonest behavior.

Make it your job to make them comprehend how things are between you and your co-parent. While your co-parent is behaving like a child, you have to keep your head up high and be the adult role model for your kids.

14. Consider parallel parenting.

If everything else fails, you may want to think about parallel parenting, which is distinct from co-parenting. You can minimize contact with your ex under this sort of agreement. Parallel parenting enables each parent to parent in the manner of their choice while the kid is in their care.

How does it work? Concerts at schools, sporting activities, and parent-teacher conferences are not events that parents attend together. Additionally, you'll probably select neutral locations for pick-ups and drop-offs from visitations. Communication only occurs when it's necessary. While the children may find this to be somewhat upsetting, it does remove parental arguments from the picture, which may be advantageous.

Even better, maybe with enough distance, you and your ex might develop greater communication and collaboration over time.

How To Set Boundaries When Co-Parenting With a Narcissist

Boundaries are a vital component of self-care that helps you to remain in control and feel secure when co-parenting with a narcissist. To establish boundaries while co-parenting with a narcissist, don't allow your ex to draw you back into their trap of gaslighting, blame, and guilt. Avoid participating in fights with the narcissist - don't feel forced to defend or justify yourself.

To prevent your ex from controlling you, don't make compromises and avoid accepting arrangements that don't work in your favor

Co-parenting with a narcissist may seem like the hardest thing imaginable. Learning what you may anticipate and how to co-parent with a narcissistic ex will help you remain in control and retain sanity.

CHAPTER TWO

Parental Alienation Syndrome

Parental alienation is the act of one parent separating their kid from the other parent through the use of tactics, which are sometimes referred to as brainwashing, alienation, or programming. Despite some disagreement regarding the phrase "parental alienation syndrome," many people use it to describe the symptoms that arise in the kid.

If your ex-spouse repeatedly and severely accuses you in front of your kid, might alienation and a related condition result?

When one parent disparages the other, the shared kid or children grow alienated. As an illustration, a mother might tell her child that their father doesn't want to talk to or see them. Or a dad tells his child that their mom prefers her new family (and kids with a new partner) over them.

Accusations might be light, or they can become fairly serious. No matter how amazing their connection was in the past, this impacts the child's image of the separated parent.

Whether the claims are true or false, the relationship between the parent and the kid suffers. Even if it's not true, if a child is repeatedly told that their father is a bad person and doesn't want to see them, for example, the child might eventually refuse to speak with or see their father when the chance arises.

The parent who is being disparaged is often referred to as the alienated parent, while the parent who is the subject of the criticism is the alienator.

Parental Alienation Syndrome Signs And Symptoms

1. The kid is undertaking what is known as a "campaign of denigration" against the estranged parent, which is persistent and unjust criticism (referred to as a "campaign of denigration")
2. The child's statements are baseless or backed up by credible facts, persuasive examples, or compelling arguments.
3. There are no redeeming characteristics to be identified; the child solely has unfavorable thoughts toward the estranged parent. This is also referred to as "lack of ambivalence" sometimes.
4. The child claims that all of the criticisms are their assessments generated from independent thought. (In PA, it is argued that the kid is "programmed" with these notions by the alienating parent.)
5. The child has unflinching support for the alienator.
6. The child doesn't feel terrible about acting poorly toward the distant parent.

7. The child alludes to events that either never occurred or happened before the child's recollection using terminology and sentences that appear to have been acquired from adult language.
8. The child's emotions of animosity against the estranged parent extend to other members of that parent's family (for example, grandparents or cousins on that side of the family), (for example, grandparents or cousins on that side of the family) (for example, grandparents or cousins on that side of family) (for example, grandparents or cousins on that side of the family).

Signs That Parental Alienation May Be Taking Place

- A child could be made aware of unnecessary relationship information by an alienator, such as instances of affairs. Undoubtedly, this might lead to the child feeling alone and angry over (or personally impacted by) something that was really between their parents.

- The alienator may prevent a child from speaking to or seeing the other parent while making it seem as if the alienated is preoccupied, busy, or disinterested in the child.
- Regardless of how much time a kid spends with the other parent, an alienator may request that all of the child's personal belongings be kept at the alienator's home.
- An alienator could routinely budge or reject custody limitations that have been established in or out of court. On the other side, an alienator can also be unwilling to make concessions about a custody plan. For instance, if the child's father is an alienator and the mom's birthday falls on a day when the dad has custody, he can vehemently reject her request to have the child join her for supper on her special day.

- There might be a rise in secrecy. There are many ways this might occur: The alienator could conceal information about the child's friends, medical records, school records, and more. This might lead the child to become estranged from the other parent since let's face it, you'll prefer to talk to the parent who knows everything about your friends, interests, and activities.
- Additionally, gossip may spread and be linked to concealment. The parent who is alienating the child could ask the child questions about their relationship and other topics. The subject of rumors might then arise from this. Oh, your father has a new partner? Who is she like? I wonder whether it will endure long. When you were in kindergarten, dad had four girlfriends, but we were still married.
- When it comes to the child's relationship with the other parent, the alienator could start to exert

control. The alienator could, for instance, make an effort to keep tabs on all encounters or phone cal s.
- One parent may be purposefully compared to a new spouse by the alienator. The child may experience this by learning that their stepmom loves them more than their mother. Even a child's stepparent would adopt them and give them a new last name that might be disclosed to them.

How Parental Alienation Affects Children

Children who experience parental alienation may develop behaviors similar to the alienator as adults.

Children who don't live with either parent may:

- feel more and more irritated
- have intensified feelings of being neglected (or perhaps having their basic needs disregarded while being caught up in their parent's fight)

- establish a bad habit that they pass on to other people
- acquire a distorted view of reality and develop a propensity for lying about other people
- become unfriendly to others as a result of adopting a "we vs. them" mentality
- consider everything to be quite "black and white"
- lack empathy

Naturally, there should be restrictions or a complete ban on exposure to a parent if they are abusive or otherwise harmful to the child. However, when two parents started as a couple and were involved in their child's upbringing, the child benefits the most from having both parents in their life after a divorce.

Children are strong. However, they are also susceptible. Children are more vulnerable when parental alienation is present.

How To Overcome Parental Alienation: Reestablishing Contact With Your Children

It might be challenging to raise a child who has been socialized to believe that you are bad or worse. What should you do if your child appears to detest you or won't come to visit? These are the five best methods for Targeted Parents to get back in touch with their kids.

1. Address exaggerations and slander.

Targeted Parents are seriously harmed by the conventional advice to "speak nothing" in the face of criticism. You must resist propaganda. Why should you remain silent when your child says to you: "Mommy claims you wanted the divorce because you don't love us? You wouldn't smile and say nothing if you were accused of murder, would you? Don't respond negatively; but, neutrally do state the truth: "I'm sorry Mommy told you that because it's not true. There was nothing personal about the divorce; it was a matter for adults. Be ready to say, "I will always love you and I will always be your daddy." [We're using "Mommy" as an example, but "Daddy" would work just as well.]

2. Encourage your child to communicate with you directly.

Parental alienation behaves in cult-like ways. For the child to hear only the Alienating Parent's (AP) perverted reality and come to believe that it is The Truth, the AP removes the child from the Targeted Parent (TP). How would you approach this? Tell your child to come to you if they have any questions about anything they've heard about you or anything they think they know about you that makes them uncomfortable. All children, regardless of whether they come from intact or divorced homes, need to learn how to approach their parents directly rather than using the other as a middleman. Even if your child doesn't believe you, at least they are hearing your side of the story, which can seem more believable to them as they get older and develop critical thinking skills.

3. Control your emotional reaction.

When you're routinely mocked and slandered by an ex who can't control their emotions, it's normal to feel enraged, afraid, and defensive. But you must make an effort to control your emotions while you're around your children. If your ex warns your kids that you're dangerous and you respond by acting frightening (for example, by losing your temper and snapping), you'll just be confirming your ex's skewed perception of events. Seek assistance if you find yourself becoming out of control via counseling, meditation, exercise, writing, etc. And keep saying it: It doesn't matter what my ex thinks of me.

4. Keep reaching out.

Continue attempting to establish a relationship with your child even if you no longer have custody of him or if he refuses your visits. Send a birthday present, text, phone, and attend events at the school. You shouldn't anticipate getting a polite response or even anyone at all. Don't interpret a lack of response, however, as a sign that your child doesn't care that you're making an effort to raise him. Even though your kid insists he doesn't want to see you and that he hates you, he surely does and is trying to test your resolve. When adult PA children meet up with a Targeted Parent, they often enquire about their disappearance and confess that they had been hoping to be "rescued" from the AP. Keep in mind to concentrate on your objective rather than the result when you are sick of your child's rejection.

5. Be tolerant.

It takes time to repair your relationship with your child; it won't happen overnight. Before you see the results of your efforts, it might take years or even until they are adults. In the meanwhile, try to let go of worrying about the result and concentrate on your desire to reconnect.

CHAPTER THREE

How to Support Your Children When Their Parent Is Narcissistic

1. Be the calm parent for your kids.

A divorce is likely to intensify feelings and undoubtedly bring out some of your spouse's narcissistic traits.

Even if you will be going through a difficult period, someone has to think for the kids. It will be your responsibility to keep them calm and secure.

That entails regulating your rage and making an effort to restrain your emotions around them. Don't make them deal with two irate parents when they already have one.

2. Avoid Being Trapped By Narcissistic Parents

The narcissist wants to elicit an emotional response from you. They want you to behave irrationally so they can portray you as the terrible parent and play the victim. Keep your emotions under control and focus on what is best for your kids.

Bringing your narcissistic parents down to their level will only lessen the impact of their conduct in the eyes of the court and your kids.

3. Limit Your Interactions While Parenting

Limit the number of times you phone or text your kids as long as you believe they are secure.

allow the kid to contact you or create a fixed time for calls. In exchange for the kid's promise that they would be allowed to communicate with you, this restricts your engagement with the narcissistic parent when calls are made to reach the child.

This is less of a problem if the child is old enough to have a mobile phone.

4. Limit your interactions with the narcissistic parent in front of the kids.

Long after the divorce is finalized, a narcissist will attempt to prolong the fight. They will try to maintain that emotional influence over you if you let them into your life and your mind.

By limiting your communication to only the kids, you can prevent this. Keep all correspondence in writing, and steer clear of off-topic topics. Ignore it if it's not about the kids.

You may provide your children more security and stability by avoiding continual disagreement.

5. Give Your Kids Recognition

Narcissists are quite skilled at making you believe that your emotions are invalid. Children are particularly vulnerable to harm from this.

Let your kids know that you see and hear them and that their feelings are real without denigrating the narcissistic parent.

Having that support from you might make it easier for them to cope with being rejected by the narcissistic parent.

6. Be careful not to criticize your ex in front of your kids.

Your children may seem to be grown up, but they are not biologically capable of carrying the weight of serving as your therapist.

Remember that even if the narcissist's actions may be abhorrent, the kid still loves them. Speaking poorly of the other parent of your kid is never acceptable. even if what you say is accurate.

7. Don't Let The Narcissist Abuse Your Child Physically Or Emotionally

You must act if you see or discover that the narcissistic parent is abusing your kid. Protecting your kid is your responsibility, and failing to do so makes you just as culpable as the abuser.

How To Protect Your Children From a Parent Who Is a Narcissist

1. Document Misconduct

Narcissists are excellent at presenting themselves to the court as perfect parents. Before the court or authorities will take any action, you will often require written documentation of the abuse.

The scenario will determine the best method for documentation. You may approach it correctly with guidance from a narcissistic divorce attorney.

2. Abide with court orders

If you are being represented by an attorney with expertise in narcissistic divorce, they would have most likely made sure that court orders had clauses that helped limit the abuse of the children by the narcissistic parent.

Typical provisions that I recommend include:

- Counseling for the kid or even joint therapy sessions with the narcissistic parent and child might help mend the connection. Even if counseling is the only way the court will let a narcissist see the kid, keep in mind that many of them will refuse to go.
- terms that forbid parents from criticizing one another in front of the kid. This may even include keeping the youngster from being disparaged by the narcissistic parent.
- clauses that forbid using physical punishment as a form of discipline.

- In certain situations, supervised visits could be necessary.

Court orders are mandatory, and disobeying them carries repercussions. Loss of custody or access to the kid may occur if a custody order is broken.

You must ensure that court orders be executed if a narcissistic parent is disobeying them. If you do nothing, you will share responsibility for your child's unfavorable outcomes.

This doesn't imply that you must report every little infraction, but you must make sure the order is followed if it endangers your kid.

CHAPTER FOUR

How To Help Your Kid Become Resilient While Co-Parenting With a Narcissist

The rest of this chapter will help you co-parent with a narcissist by examining how resilience may be developed and fostered in kids to shield them from the narcissist's potentially destructive behavior.

Keep in mind that you cannot alter the narcissist's behavior or personality. So, how can you strike a balance between co-parenting and ensuring the safety of your kids? In most cases, the solution consists in helping kids develop their resilience.

Resilience is the capacity to bounce back swiftly from setbacks and obstacles, as well as the ability to function despite them. Resilience in children starts to develop at a very early age. Parents may help children build resilience in a variety of ways.

1. Being their safe base

First off, by giving kids a safe and secure "base" to come back to while they explore and discover the world. Allowing your kid to go out into the world, or in this instance, visit the narcissistic parent, and then being the calm, safe, and secure place to which they return, is part of having this safe foundation. This is no simple task. It asks you to temporarily set aside your feelings to listen to your kid and consider anything they may be telling you about what occurred while they were with their other parent.

2. Foster a strong sense of identity

A child's sense of self, identity, and self-worth plays a key role in resilience. The goal is to give your kid some autonomy in their lives and to give them chances to show responsibility.

3. internal locus of control

To increase confidence and self-belief, it's also important to promote learning new abilities. The kid learns that they can affect external occurrences rather than thinking the contrary, which is often the result of narcissistic abuse, and this also promotes an internal locus of control.

4. Discernment

They become more resilient when their discernment and capacity to reject self-defeating messages are supported, which in turn equips them with crucial abilities for managing their relationship with their narcissistic parent.

5. Direction

Children must also have hope for the future and a feeling of purpose in life. Setting goals and encouraging your kids to have ambitions are two ways to do this.

6. Demonstrating effective communication

Last but not least, kids must have access to other positive interactions outside their parents. A spiritual guide, a teacher at school, an aunt, or an uncle might be this. Children learn to establish their boundaries and know what to anticipate when it comes to their through developing strong and supportive social networks and modeling healthy, respectful relationships.

Resilience is crucial while co-parenting with a narcissist.

Your children will have more control in their interactions with their narcissistic parents if you help them develop resilience. They learn about their value as a result, and they become less susceptible to deception.

Resilience will enable children to politely advocate for themselves as they become older and prevent them from maybe forming problematic relationships.

In the end, it comes down to equipping them with the life skills they will need to preserve healthy boundaries with their narcissistic parent long into adulthood and when they start their own families.

Made in United States
Troutdale, OR
02/14/2025